GOLF
SECRETS
OF THE
PROS

A DAVID & CHARLES BOOK
Copyright David & Charles Limited 2010

David & Charles is an F+W Media Inc. company
4700 East Galbraith Road
Cincinnati, OH 45236

First published in 2010

GOLF
WORLD

Source material courtesy of *Golf World* magazine © Bauer Consumer Media

A catalogue record for this book is available from the British Library.

ISBN-13: 978-0-7153-3612-0 flexibound
ISBN-10: 0-7153-3612-6 flexibound

Printed in China by Toppan Leefung Printing Limited
for David & Charles
Brunel House, Newton Abbot, Devon

Commissioning Editor: Neil Baber
Assistant Editor: James Brooks
Design Manager: Sarah Clark
Art Editor: Charly Bailey
Project Editor: Duncan Lennard
Production Controller: Kelly Smith

Visit our website at www.davidandcharles.co.uk

David & Charles books are available from all good bookshops; alternatively you
can contact our Orderline on 0870 9908222 or write to us at FREEPOST
EX2 110, D&C Direct, Newton Abbot, TQ12 4ZZ (no stamp required UK only);
US customers call 800-289-0963 and Canadian customers call 800-840-5220.

GOLF

SECRETS
OF THE
PROS

THE WORLD'S TOP
PLAYERS REVEAL
THEIR WINNING TIPS

David and Charles

EDITED BY DUNCAN LENNARD

CONTENTS

Introduction   06

THE POWER ZONE   08
FINDING THE GREEN   30
THE SCORE ZONE   52
SAND SECRETS   78
ON THE GREEN   98
BEATING PRESSURE   116
TOUR TECHNIQUE   128

Player Guide   156
Index   160

INTRODUCTION

I was once asked to write an instructional article with a former European Ryder Cup player on striking a bunker shot from a downhill lie. Perched on the slope, the player was popping the ball out next to the pin time and again. When I asked him how he did it, he looked at me like I just asked him to explain how his central nervous system worked. 'I don't know,' he shrugged, at last. 'I just do it.'

It's stories like this that help build the myth that Tour pros are not very good at giving instruction. Supposedly they are either so naturally gifted that they have no concept of how to break technique down and coach it – as per our Ryder Cup friend; or, they are working on techniques so advanced that their knowledge is of little relevance to us ordinary mortals. Happily the theory is like a USGA-spec green – it holds very little water. The Tour pro makes an excellent coach – a fact underlined many times throughout the pages of *Golf Secrets of the Pros*.

For a start, that talent-blessed pro who plays the game naturally is gratifyingly rare. Yes, they exist; but the vast majority of Tour pros learned the game like you and me, through a mixture of coaching, technical

information, trial-and-error and downright hard work. The very process of grinding a technique out of the dirt has given them expert and privileged knowledge of what makes a golf swing tick – knowledge they share with you here.

As for the 'they-play-a-different-game' theory, well, Tour pros may be approaching super-human status, but they are yet to discover a way to bend the laws of physics to suit their game. The factors governing a successful shot for them are the same as for us – angle of attack, face angle at impact, swing path at impact. Go to the range at any European Tour event and you will see the world's elite working on the same basics – grip, ball position, stance, alignment – that your club pro would coach you on a Saturday morning.

That's not to say that the Tour pro does not also find ways to make his game technically advanced; it's just that he puts the foundations in place first. Take for example the chapter on sand play. In one section we have Swedish Ryder Cup star Henrik Stenson revealing a fascinating trap technique that shuns the traditional out-to-in cut in favour of a straighter swing which

stops the ball kicking right
– while in another, India's
Jeev Milkha Singh runs through
the five essentials that all
bunker players must adopt.
They may represent different
levels of technique, but both are relevant
and, above all, useful.

In this way, *Golf Secrets of the Pros*
takes you right through the game from the
tee peg to the bottom of the cup, with the
likes of Padraig Harrington, Lee Westwood,
Paul Casey and Ian Poulter lining up to give
you the benefit of their experience. There
are also special sections on dealing with
pressure – after all, it's a way of life for those
guys – and, for the technophiles among you,
Tour technique.

The information in these pages will not
turn you into a Tour pro – for that you need
to spend a few years at the range – but it
will give you a much better understanding
of both the building blocks that create a
pro golf swing, and the hidden methods
that can take it to an advanced level. At the
very least, it should give you some excellent
avenues to explore as the quest to improve
your game continues.

THE POWER ZONE

Modern, powerful equipment and ever-lengthening courses have turned golf into a power game, with distance off the tee an increasingly valuable weapon. Here, the European Tour's elite share their secrets on the yard-munching techniques they use to propel the ball more than 300 yards on a regular basis — and without sacrificing control.

DRIVE WITH POWER AND ACCURACY

A mixture of great technique and physical strength have made Paul Casey one of the longest and straightest drivers of the golf ball in the game. Here, Casey and coach Peter Kostis describe the keys to his swing and explain what you can take from them.

1 At address

My ball position is on the left heel. My spine is tilted to the right and my weight is evenly balanced.

2 The takeaway

I make sure all parts of my body start to move at the same time. Hands, arms, shoulders, and hips all start turning simultaneously.

3 Top of the backswing

I've retained the flex in my right knee and a release of my left knee has allowed the left thigh to move behind the ball. This classic power position helps me get ready for the transition to the downswing.

4 The start of the downswing

I re-plant my left heel to put my left leg in position to accept the swing coming forward. The belt buckle is facing the ball, yet my shoulders are still closed. Creating this separation between hips and shoulders allows me to retain a powerful 90° angle between the club's shaft and my arms.

5 Coming down

I'm rotating my chest and shoulders, yet still almost retaining the 90°angle between the club's shaft and my arms. This is where so much of the power comes from. I've driven with my legs and the hips have turned, driving the left shoulder up and back. The key is to feel like both body and club are moving through the hitting area together.

Pro Secrets

In practice, Paul picks his left foot up on the backswing and hovers it next to his right shoe. He returns it to its original position on the way down. This helps transfer his weight and smoothes his first move down.

6 Just after impact

I control the power as my right heel is not way off the ground. I've generated as much power as I can without getting my body out of position.

7 The finish

This classic follow-through sees no 'reverse C'. I'm not lunging forward with my upper body. I've swung on to my left side, but not past it.

AT THE TOP
FAST AND STRONG...

For the past nine years Casey and Kostis have been working on areas to make his swing simpler, more consistent and more repetitive. 'One of the things I stress with all of my students,' says Kostis, 'is to make the swing fit their bodies and then to make their bodies fit their swings. Paul has tremendously strong arms and so he can generate a lot of controlled speed in his swing. Someone with less strength would lose the control.'

Rhythm
Your tempo can only be as fast as you have the strength to control. Within that, you must pick a rhythm to match your personality.

Right knee brace
I always brace my right knee and swing around it. When things used to go wrong, it was usually because my right leg would straighten at the top of the backswing, which would restrict my turn.

Left heel can lift
Some teachers would tell you this heel coming off the ground is 'old school' but I'm a firm believer that if you want to generate power and consistency it's very difficult to do with your left heel fixed to the ground.

THE FINISH
BALANCE AND CONTROL

Paul's swing used to finish with him poking his head forward, almost through an imaginary window. This has disappeared over the years and now he has a classic followthrough position, full of balance and control. 'Paul has worked very hard on his flexibility over the years,' says Kostis, 'especially in his hamstrings. This allows him to get into the right positions.'

Pro Secrets

Casey practises full swings with both feet planted on the ground. This helps him stay centred and turning properly, rather than sliding.

FIND THE FAIRWAY TO HIT MORE GREENS

My greens-in-regulation stat has always been one of my strongest, but the key to it is my driver. If you can position the tee shot well then it makes greens more accessible – plus if you're long, then you're going in with less club.

So what is the secret of long, straight driving? For me, the answer has to be rhythm. That, above anything else, is the best way to be consistent. If you can make your tempo the same each time then your shot patterns will be similar.

Having said that, there are a number of other things that I work on to help me find the cut grass. Let me show you what I mean.

Rhythm

All good drivers have good rhythm. My tempo never changes; it's built in. I tend to hit the ball straight rather than with a fade or draw.

DRILL IT DOWN THE MIDDLE

These driver swing keys can help you hit it consistently straighter.

I've noticed I lose a lot of yards when I'm driving the ball into the wind. This is because the flight has been high and stalling due to too much spin. The changes I've made have been to develop a more penetrative trajectory with less backspin, so giving me extra yards in all conditions.

Set the wrists early

In the takeaway, you want to see the club move first. if you get too much shoulder turn too early, then halfway back they have nowhere else to go, except over-turning. A drill I often use on the range to combat this is pre-setting the full wrist cock early in the backswing. I'm prone to getting a little outside the line on the takeaway (inset) so this helps me to rehearse a better move away from the ball.

Left arm plane checkpoint

Another checkpoint comes midway through the backswing. I'm looking to keep my left arm working up and around rather than getting across my chest. It keeps my swing on a better plane, which helps accuracy.

FROM THE TOP
TO THE BALL

Down the line

I'm looking to get the clubshaft pointing more at the target at the top with a little more angle in my left wrist position. I have tended to get a touch laid off with the back of the left wrist too flat. With the club pointing left of the target at the top (inset), the ball starts further left than I would want and fades back, which isn't a terrible shot, but it's not what I'm looking for. If I don't get my hands high enough at the top of the backswing, my arms lag behind my body and then, as they start to catch up, I get a little bit steep on the ball.

Bow and arrow

My left shoulder is too low here. This means to square the club up and hit it flush and arrow-straight, I have to keep the left arm bent.

My bent left arm

The fact I hit the ball with a bowed left arm is something that people always talk about in connection with my swing. It's an idiosyncrasy of mine and something I've always done. The reason it stays bowed is because I lean into the shot too much, get a little steep and the arm doesn't have time to extend.

Built to fade

On the plus side, my left arm stops me hitting it left because it doesn't rotate as it should. It means I'm comfortable with a fade. I have to work hard to draw the ball, by staying back and getting the club more inside the line.

To correct this bowed left arm I work on staying behind the ball more and turning through it rather than leaning. If I can do this, my left shoulder rises – putting my arm in a more traditional impact position.

CONSISTENCY – IN TWO EASY STAGES

I'm longer than I was. Some of it is down to the extra time I've spent in the gym; but what interests me is that I get more clubhead speed when I don't swing the club back so far. Not only that – a more compact swing boosts consistency too.

I'm posing this position because this is where I like to imagine the club finishing at the top of the backswing; in reality, my momentum will allow the club to reach horizontal. My shoulders have turned 90° and I'm fully coiled. From here I can drop the club down and on plane as I move into the ball.

Because I'm quite flexible, I can turn my shoulders past 90° (above); but when I do this I feel like my hands get too far behind me. They can get caught too much on the inside on the way down, and then the club is off plane. I have to save the shot with the hands through the ball.

If you start the downswing properly then this position – shaft pointing to your target when horizontal – is easy to find and the perfect one to get into. If you can find this position on the way to the ball, then you can't hit a wayward shot.

I'm showing you this so you can picture what you need to do. Work on staging the position for yourself, because you can't think about moving into this position when you're actually swinging the club because it all happens too quickly. The club should be parallel to the ground, just ahead of the toes with the butt end pointing at the target.

HITTING THE DRAW
OFF THE TEE

I've always hit a nice high draw, something which helped me win the 1991 Masters as many holes at Augusta dogleg right-to-left. But the draw, with its distance advantage, is a useful shot to have on any course. Here's how I do it.

stand tall
Maintaining height is crucial for any shot, but when you're trying for a wide, low arc it's essential to retain your height.

Using the tee
I was always taught to tee up on the side of where the trouble is. If you want to hit a draw, like at the 10th, where it's so bloody tight and you really have to whip it round, you have to get far right on the tee to help get round the corner.

rotate arms
Rolling the hands over to release the clubhead helps maximise the distance on the shot and ensure the draw. It should feel like a shot you might play in squash or tennis.

Pro Secrets
If you have missed the fairway, be realistic about what you can do from the rough. So many amateurs stride into the rough holding a 3-wood when I'm thinking 9-iron.

Set-up: use your alignment

For me, the draw all about the stance and the ball position rather than anything complicated. I aim the face where I want the ball to finish and the feet and shoulders to the right. Take it away on the inside and simply swing along your foot line.

Eyes Right

I look at the back of the ball. It brings the hips forward and promotes a wider, shallower swing.

High or Low

For a low draw, move the ball back in your stance; for more height go forwards. Keep it simple.

Tee height

Work around the wind by teeing it higher downwind and lower, to penetrate, when hitting into it.

CHASING THE RAINBOW

Solid address

Make sure you are lined up parallel to the target line. That means your feet, knees, hips and shoulders should all be parallel. I like a nice, stable, fairly wide stance, feet just wider than shoulders. Finally, I like the ball just inside my left heel.

Hinge and turn

The crucial move for me is to let the club hinge and turn early on the inside. If I have a fault it is moving the club outside the line, so this thought actually gets me to move the club straight up the line. From here I can pre-set the club early.

On line at the top

At the top of the takeaway I am trying to get the club as close to the down-the-line position as possible.

The Ryder Cup star reveals the six swing positions he uses to help him achieve the so-called rainbow trajectory – high launch, low-spin – which delivers your maximum yardage.

Early release

I try to release the club early on the way down. It's vital to create a wide arc if you want to maximise your power. Releasing the club early into the impact position keeps the arc wide and boosts your swing force.

On the up at impact

Try and hit the ball slightly on the up. Not only does this take some of the backspin off; it maximises your launch angle. Your ball will take off higher, and the optimal spin to give a high, hanging ball flight.

Balanced finish

It's important to just let your finish happen naturally; all you need to make sure is that you are in a balanced position at the end.

DRIVING ON A LINKS

Links golf presents specific problems to your tee game. Pot bunkers, sometimes in the fairway, strong winds and knee-high grass are just three problems you need to take into account. The secret, which worked so well for me in my 2007 and 2008 Open wins, is to prioritise keeping the ball in play. Do that, and you give yourself a tremendous advantage.

Do you need to be long?
No, because on a links course the ball runs. You need to be effective, which means getting the right shape relative to the wind to get the most out of your tee shots.

Work your driver
On a links, you need to be able to work the driver to hold the ball against the wind. If you let it go with the wind then it's going to run until it finds a trap.

Avoid the sand
... at all costs. If that means hitting a longer shot into a green then so be it. On links courses the bunker is tantamount to a penalty shot. I'll risk going into the rough rather than finding a bunker.

Tee it higher
When playing a drive downwind I'm trying to get a bit more distance out of it, but in some ways I'm not all that conscious of it. I'll basically just move the ball forward in my stance and tee it a little higher, so that I can catch it more on the upswing. Such a drive is more likely to fly with a little fade.

Time for a change
I changed my driver before Carnoustie 2007, reducing the loft from 9.5° to 8.5° and the length by 2in to 46. Those moves gave me the extra control I needed on a tough driving course.

○ ALVARO QUIROS

HOW TO HIT A 300-YARD DRIVE

I have always been near or at the top of the European Tour stats for power, and average over 300 yards. Perhaps it's the fact that I have very long arms which give me added leverage... or perhaps it was because my father gave me a very long and very heavy club to practise with when I was learning to play.

I do remember, though, getting to about 17 years old and suddenly realising that I was flying the ball much further than I'd ever done before. It was almost a click-of-the-fingers thing. One minute I was average and then I woke up and was launching it miles.

Whatever it is, there is no getting away from the fact that natural length gives you a great advantage in today's game. The old guys are right – the game is easier with all the new equipment and the skill factor has been reduced. But there are still things you can work on to boost your power. By explaining where I feel my power comes from, I hope you can add some distance to your drives too.

The first metre matters

Everything about the swing should be synchronised so that no part of the action gets ahead or left behind. That's why my first thought on the practice ground is to make sure that I start everything together.

For the first metre back, I've kept everything together to make sure that my shoulders, arms, body and club all have a part to play from the start.

Focus on the shaft

I've fitted an Aldila Voodoo shaft in my driver; it takes off spin and gives me a lower flight. The shaft you use can have a drastic effect on your game.

At the top of the backswing I want to be fully loaded with my shoulders turned 90° and the club in, or just over, the horizontal position.

Once I've completed the first metre, then I'm looking to get the wrists fully cocked as I take the club to the top.

The writing on the glove

See here what I have written on my glove? It says 'Taco + Arriba'. That is telling me to get my hands fully cocked and up. I'll often write a thought on my glove; I think it helps to play with some kind of simple trigger in your head when you're on the course. I try not to think about any technique when I'm playing.

Start with the hands

They say the swing starts from the ground up, but that doesn't help me at all. By far the most important thing in the transition for me is to START WITH THE HANDS. That's because I have a tendency to slide the hips forwards too early; then my hands and arms can't catch up and I can lose the shot to the right.

You can see here how the body has been too active and left the hands behind. I've lost the width here and the tempo is too explosive from the top.

X

You get no prizes for trying to rip into it from here. Apply the power too soon and you'll lose power at impact, as well as control. Notice I've kept the width in my swing. My hands have stayed away from my chest. If I go too quickly with my body, then I can get narrow, which leads to inconsistency.

I try to imagine the club coming down on the same plane that it went back. In reality this doesn't happen, but the thought is a good one. My bad habit is to drop the club onto a much flatter plane. It means the club lags behind and I get too active with the hands.

Extend through impact

One thought I have is to try and keep the hands as close to the target line as I can as I'm striking the ball.

Turn the left hip for power

I look to turn my left hip away so that I then have the space to swing the club. This turning of the hip is also a great source of power, but it must be synchronised with the natural swing. Don't go twisting out of the way too early or it'll throw your arms and hands outside the line.

That's a metre before and after impact. Don't pull the club to the inside too fast; feel yourself reach for the target with your right hand.

Hitting up against a wall is a great image; it makes you stay high with your left shoulder and it means you have stayed just behind the ball at impact.

FINDING THE GREEN

Tour statistics show an impressive correlation between finding the green in regulation and winning the tournament. That's why Tour pros spend so much time working on controlling shape, trajectory and distance with their irons. Use this wealth of green-finding keys and you can't help but increase your birdie opportunities -- and your trophy count.

CONTROL YOUR SHOT SHAPE

1. RIGHT AT IT

Before we move on to shaping the ball, let's not forget that sometimes what's needed is an iron shot that covers the flag all the way. It's an aggressive play and needs confidence to pull it off – but it's a useful one to have.

Start on plane...

The key is to keep the club on plane through the swing; it allows you to swing straight down the line. Maintain a solid posture going away from the ball; then look to find this neutral position, clubshaft in line with one across your toes, as you return into the ball.

...and stay there

See here how the clubhead mirrors the position it achieved on the downswing? The shaft is not exactly parallel to the shafts on the ground because the hands remain slightly inside the line, but it is very close.

On a par 3, you don't need to tee the ball high. Think of it more like getting an ideal lie on the ground. The best iron strikes are when you squeeze down, rather than sweeping it away like a driver.

I find it helps to pick a spot just in front of me on the target line to aim over. But this isn't just an alignment aid because I also use it to encourage a full release down the line of the shot.

Alignment aids

I carry the yellow sticks you can see on these pages with me everywhere. They are ideal for practising alignment and giving you a visual aid. Set up with everything square and then check your positions using the guides.

2. FADE IT

The soft high fade

The high fade is not a tough shot to play, but it still needs practice to add the control you need. Play the shot with an open stance, but aim the clubface at the target before you grip it. Just swing on a line with your shoulders and release normally. To the player, it looks here like the ball has moved back in the stance, but it hasn't really – all I've done is draw the left foot back into the open stance.

Open stance

You can see here how I've set up to the left and have swung the club along my shoulder and feet line.

Moving the ball left-to-right is a shot many amateurs know very well. But if you want to play precision golf, you can adapt the shape to suit the shot. You may need a high floater to a tight pin or a low, drilled shot that runs a little more when it hits the ground. Let me show you how to master both shots.

The low, power fade

From a square stance, you are looking to take the club away outside the target line and then release just inside it. Be careful not to rotate the toe of the club past the heel too soon after impact. You are squeezing the ball here with a slightly downward blow, starting it to the left of the target and then letting it drift back. This will come out low and running.

Outside
My stance is square to the target, but I'm picking the club up outside the target line.

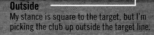

3. DRAW IT

The soft high draw

From a square stance, you are then looking to work the club back inside the line. From here, come into the ball from just inside the line and release the club outside the target line. A little rotation in the hands helps, but you do need to be swinging the club well and on a good plane to get the full benefit.

Inside
You need to route the club on the inside as you take it away...

The low running draw

The main difference is that I close my stance, but keep the club aiming at the target. This in effect de-lofts the club which means that the shot will come out lower and hotter. There is more of a squeezing effect going on here at impact as you swing along your shoulder line and across the target line. Experiment with your address to vary the amounts of spin.

Closed
I've set up here as though I'm aiming with my body to the right of where I want the ball to go.

Outside

...and then release across the target line to the outside for a gentle, high draw.

In-to-out

The clubface is still square to the target line, despite the fact that I'm swinging along the line of my feet.

37

CHEATING THE WIND

Keeping the ball below the breezes is a question of making some smart set-up adjusments.

Club Selection

Taking extra club allows you to hit the ball softer, which also makes the ball fly lower — ideal if you need control, and doubly so in the wind. A softer strike does mean less backspin, but you can accept it running on a bit in order to remove some of the doubt about the shot.

Grip Down

Controlling the ball doesn't mean you have to play an out-and-out punch shot. I would just go an inch down the grip, to keep the flight down a little and help the ball penetrate the wind.

left heel

I like to play all standard shots just inside the left heel so I get the same consistent flight with all the irons.

Strike with purpose

Drive down hard on the ball and keep the body moving through impact: it's very easy to ease off on short shots like this.

Low down

If I want to hit one a bit lower I may move it back a tad, although it then won't pitch as far and I may have to reclub accordingly.

DRILLS TO FIND MORE GREENS

Three green-finding keys –
for the course and the range

On the course

I play with a lot of swingthoughts,
but I don't use them when I'm
hitting the ball. That's why the
practice swing is so important – it
is during this motion that all the
keys are rushing through my head.
When I step over the ball, I clear my
mind from the technical stuff and
commit to the shot I've planned.

Playing under pressure is all about
working to a routine. When someone
chokes, it generally means they
haven't stuck to their routine. You
have to focus on what you're trying
to do. You have to have a clear
picture and execute the shot.

Left hand drill

One of my faults is that I ease off it and don't always hit through the ball as I should. That can lead to a pull or a cut if I hang onto it too long. A good drill for me is to simply hold the club in my left hand and complete a full swing. All the way back... and all the way through. It ensures that you make a full shoulder turn and then force your body to work all the way through to a full finish.

Rotation for a draw

I have a habit of picking the club up too steeply, which is a flaw that can lead to pulls, cuts and slices. I work on this by turning the club upside down so the toe points to the ground, and then practising the takeaway. You'll find the club tracks round more easily into a good position, in which it has rotated nicely into a slightly flatter plane away from the ball. That is ideal for a right-to-left shot.

THE ONE FOOT WAGGLE

Before I play most shots I'll draw the club away from the ball by about a foot and then return it back to address. I carry out this little routine for two reasons:
• I focus on taking the club away so that my shoulders, arms and clubhead are all that move. My hips stay very still. This is to remind me to start the swing with my upper body so that I can maximise resistance.
• Secondly, it works as a trigger that settles me down and gets me mentally ready to play the shot.
If you make a move like this before you commit to your actual swing, you'll find that you can stay a lot more smooth in the takeaway.

Check point
Use the waggle to remind you about resistance.

Hips on hold
I want to make sure my legs are passive in the backswing.

Loose limbs
This small move helps you stay fluid and ready to go.

○ PADRAIG HARRINGTON

PLAYING THE LOW PUNCH

I rarely think about technique when I'm on the course; I'll just rely on instinct picked up through years of experience. Having said that, if I want to keep the ball low there are a number of adjustments I'll make naturally. But before you work on any of these, make sure you're taking enough club for the shot. Amateurs rarely do!

Finish
Finally, I've mirrored the backswing with a three-quarter finish.

Backswing
The backswing is shorter than usual. I could say three-quarter back, but that isn't a firm rule. It's more important to swing easy.

Impact
I'm more over the ball at impact, leaning on the shot. My shoulders are squarer to the target line; I haven't turned as much as I would normally. Holding the shoulders back encourages the clubhead to close down a little so that you have a low launch angle.

Address
I've moved the ball towards the middle of my stance.

LEARN TO READ THE ROUGH

When you're in the rough you have to read the lie: which direction is the grass growing? How long is it? and most importantly, is it damp or dry? There are several factors to consider.

Dry, wispy

When you have dry, wispy rough, usually yellow in colour, you are going to get massive fliers, so I'll often take less club than I need. It might even be a club less than I'd take from the corresponding place in the fairway. On this one here, the grass is yellow, dry and it's growing the way I want to hit it. This is going to go for miles. From a lie like this, it's possible to hit an 8-iron 60 yards more than normal.

Wet and lush

This can be nasty. You need to worry about the club getting snagged up and turning over. You can see how all this grass is going to come between the club and the ball. You can't make clean contact even if you come down steeper. I might try to hit an 8-iron and I'd be trying to smash it. If the club turns over it'll go left, so to counter that I weaken my grip and hold the clubface off, relying on strength to keep it square.

TWO THOUGHTS FOR TOUGH CONDITIONS

Playing in strong winds is very difficult, but if you can focus on these two keys you can still find it possible to control your game.

Ball spin

In basic terms, the harder you hit the ball, the more spin gets put on the ball, the more lift is developed and the higher it goes. Resisting the temptation to hit harder is the key and sometimes you just have to accept that you might not be able to reach a hole that is usually within range.

Rhythm

The biggest thing to remember is rhythm: that is the magic word for amateurs and pros, and should be the only thing in your head. If you try to force the shot it will go sideways. Simply take more club, swing smoothly at 70 per cent power and you'll be able to keep the ball under the wind.

Across the grain

Just as you can get a flier when the grass grows with you, there's a chance this can jump to the right at impact because as the clubface slows down, the grass opens it up. It's impossible to make clean contact with the ball here. It's lush and damp, so you need to swing harder because the ball will come out slowly. It's a bit like a bunker shot, except you are trying at least to make contact with the ball.

THE ART OF IRON PLAY

Paul McGinley has a lovely rhythmical quality to his swing which is key to his consistency as a class ball striker.

But Paul is especially good with his irons; and this is because he gets his chest nicely over the ball. You can see that, around the top of his backswing, he's already in a decent impact position. You might expect him to have his weight a little more on the right, getting loaded behind the ball, but he actually stays quite central. This means that through impact his left knee slides outside his left foot, a sure sign that he has driven hard with his legs to get that solid, boring trajectory.

Ideally, if he had initially moved more behind the ball, then you wouldn't expect his left leg to bow towards the target quite so much.

Paul, though, has the core strength to make this work because he recovers brilliantly in the last three frames to produce a classic finishing pose.

Looking for width, Paul has quite a late wrist cock and allows his right arm to stay above his left.

The left knee moves outside his left foot because he has been so central with his weight at the top.

You can see from the building behind how Paul keeps his head very central in the takeaway.

Paul centres his chest over the ball and holds it there through impact.

Look how the right knee has worked towards the left – a classic leg action.

You can draw a straight line down from the right shoulder to the left foot in this textbook finishing pose.

CENTRE YOUR WEIGHT
FOR CONSISTENCY

The faults that you need to keep a close eye on are the ones that have troubled you since you started to play. I've always had a tendency to have my weight too much in the toes at address. It can lead to several problems as I'll explain here.

Most amateurs stand too close to the ball, but I was too far away. To reach the ball I had to stretch for it and that meant too much of my weight was on the balls of my feet. Compare my heels in this picture with the one to the right.

The result was that the takeaway was poor and I got into a terrible position at the top. The left shoulder dipped, I lifted the club up too steeply and my shoulder turn was tilted. You can see how I've stooped and lost my full height.

Here's a good position at the top. The plane is not so steep and I've maintained height. Good positions mean greater consistency.

This is much better. Puff your chest out and make sure your feet are grounded with the weight in the centre.

○ DARREN CLARKE

BARREL DRILL
SWING SEQUENCE

Darren was struggling with a swaying motion, so I made him stand in an old sherry barrel, says coach Ewen Murray. Unfortunately it was empty, but it still worked as a great visual aid and Darren

always works better if he can visualise what it is we are trying to achieve.

We used the barrel so that he could see how much he swayed his hips from side to side as he swung the club. When Darren

first gave it a go, he bumped into the sides both on the way back and coming through.

We've added lines here to replicate the edges of the barrel. You can clearly see how he now swings the club without touching

the rim. This is evidence we've got rid of the sliding and replaced it with a rotation of the hips round a more central axis. Turning the hips means he has a shallower arc and can take the club away on a much better plane.

THE SCORE ZONE

When it comes to turning three shots into two, every pro tour event is a masterclass. Here, the world's top short game exponents reveal the detail behind those eye-catching flop shots and canny bump-and-runs — and give a real insight into how the elite player seeks to harness spin to finesse the ball next to the hole time and again.

○ **DARREN CLARKE**
LEARN TO LOVE YOUR WEDGE

How accurate are you with your wedges? How often do you hit the ball close enough to the hole to give yourself a real chance to score? When I asked myself those questions, the answer I came up with was 'not often enough'. So I headed back to the drawing board and came up with five key points to make my wedge game, and hopefully yours, a real weapon on the golf course.

1. MOVE YOUR HANDS FORWARD AT ADDRESS

Old

I used to hit the ball too high with my wedge, which meant I was struggling to control my distance — something which must be spot-on if you want to pitch close consistently. De-lofting the club at address is the first move to improving the penetration in the flight. Move your hands forward, but make sure the face remains square to the target.

Full face
Keep the clubhead square for consistent results off the face.

Hands ahead
Although my grip looks weaker, I haven't changed the position of my hands on the club at all.

Pro Secrets
If the pin is at the front of the green, I'll hit my sand iron so I can stop it or spin it back. With the pin at the back, I will look to run the ball up the green.

2. RETAIN THE ANGLE

This is the most important factor of all – keeping the angle between the right forearm and the shaft through impact. My trajectory is now much lower than it has been before. If the initial trajectory is good then it's much easier to control distance, especially in the wind.

Drive with the body - not the hands
You need to hit down on the ball to make it go up. So if your hands are a little active, that's a useful thing to remember. You need to take some sort of divot.

Right angle
By posing the impact position here, I can show you how the angle of the right wrist is maintained from set-up (above right), keeping the same amount of loft on the club.

Pro Secrets
If you want to hit the ball harder, try using your body more. The arms follow the body and the hands follow the arms.

Choke down for greater control
If most amateurs just choked down the club a little more for shots around the green, it would help them a lot. When you have 60 to 80 yards to go, drop an inch or so down the shaft – it's much easier and you get greater control.

3. BALL POSITION GOVERNS HEIGHT

Stop dead

Whether I'm punching it in a little low or not, I'd expect the reaction on the green to be the same: one bounce and stop. If I wanted to run the ball up the green, I'd take one more club and hit it easier.

Middle

Back

If you want to hit the ball even lower, then just move it back in the stance. But when you're faced with a wedge into the wind, don't fall into the trap of trying to hit the ball harder. If you force this shot, you'll add spin and your hopes of keeping the ball low are lost.

What's more, into a breeze it's crucial to hold that angle in the back of the right wrist through impact. This can be hard to do if you swing too powerfully, owing to centrifugal force, but if you can maintain that angle then the ball can't go high.

Cut off

I would generally only swing three-quarter length into a strong wind. See here how I've curtailed the follow through.

Avoid thrash, adopt smooth

Amateurs try to hit wedges too hard. The pros, from a 7-iron upwards, will often swing at 75 per cent because they are trying to take spin off the ball. With wedges, too much spin is the enemy — we want to stop the ball where it lands. My advice for all club players would be to take one more club and learn to play with more control.

4. KEEP THE SHOULDERS LEVEL

Bad position is left shoulder down. This also encourages a reverse pivot which gets your weight working in the wrong way – forwards then back.

Your swing will naturally be a little steeper with the wedge, but don't get too steep. Try and keep the shoulders level because this will help you to keep a consistent strike.

I used to start the swing too much with my hands and because they were behind the ball, the shaft would go away first. I then had to re-route and end up compensating with my hands – never a good thing. Now I keep everything on plane and in sync.

5. KEEP TURNING

Stop on this shot and you're dead. If your
body stops turning, you'll get steep, the club
will take a huge divot and the results...well,
they'll be inconsistent at best.

Stay shallow

With the hands forward, you MUST
turn through the shot, so that the
base of the swing stays shallow
enough to take a small divot.

MAKE SPIN YOUR FRIEND

I tend to spin the ball a lot, so when I'm about 100 yards out I have a few options. I can throw the ball past the hole and spin it back, or I can choose a lower flight and stop the ball where it lands. Here's how I approach both.

Option 1: spin it back

With plenty of green behind the flag, I would usually take my sand wedge, which is 56 degrees, and spin the ball back. To make that happen, I may move the ball back a fraction and I'll be aggressive through impact. That means holding the club off as long as I can before releasing hard through the ball. This ensures a steep angle of attack and plenty of action. Just look at the divot!

Pitch perfect #1

When there's room behind the hole, you can zip the ball back.

Relax to boost accuracy

For club players who struggle with their wedges, the two words I think are important are Relax and Release. If you get tense with a wedge, your chances of hitting it straight are not good. Try to flow through impact and concentrate on a balanced finish. Here are two other hints that will help:

• **Accuracy.** Aim at a point about a foot ahead of the ball and hit over that. I've popped a tee peg in here, to give you the idea. I might aim at a bare patch in the grass or some kind of blemish.

• **Distance.** I gauge distance by the speed of my swing, not the length of it. The length is pretty constant, but I'll have an 80-yard speed or a 100-yard speed.

Option 2: hit and hold

Stopping the ball in its tracks is good if the pin is at the back of the green. I'll take a pitching wedge with only 48 degrees of loft and play a different shot. This is a slower tempo with a much quieter release, just bumping the ball forward with a less pronounced divot. You still need to be firm, but the ball flight will be lower and the ball will spin just enough to stop on landing.

Pitch perfect #2

See how the control on this shot keeps the ball very quiet on landing.

THE LOB SHOT:
IT'S ALL A QUESTION OF BOUNCE

I often see amateurs attempting to hit a high floater with a lob wedge that has 10 degrees of bounce, but if you try that, you're asking for trouble.

My Titleist lob wedge has just four degrees, enabling it to slip under the ball more easily. I get noticeably more spin with this club than an ordinary wedge. So don't try high lobs off tight lies if your club is not set up for it.

To play this shot, you need to commit fully and have fast hands. My feet are close together and my weight favours the left side from start to finish.

1 It's a longer swing...

2 ... Be fast at the bottom...

3 ... And allow the clubhead to overtake the hands.

GREENSIDE FINESSE

Cutting the ball up into the air off a tight lie is one of golf's scarier shots – unfortunately, it's also one of the game's most needed. Use these tips to build your own confidence.

Pro Secrets

The tighter the lie, the less bounce you can afford to use. For example I normally have 6, 7, or 8 degrees but at Augusta it goes down to 4 because the lies there are so tight.

Hold the face open

I try to keep the clubface open through impact and beyond – that naturally leads to an abbreviated followthrough. If the face was a mirror, you should be able to see your face in it after impact.

The set-up

The simple idea is that I point the club where I want the ball to land. Everything else – feet, knees, shoulders – is wide open and pointing left of the target. The ball is forward in the stance. This promotes a high shot.

The strike

Ideally you are trying to cut across the ball and put as much spin on it as possible. Try not to get too steep on the ball. You want to try to slide the blade smoothly underneath the ball.

YOUR PRIVATE LESSON IN THE ART OF CHIPPING

Adam Scott's chipping game has improved by 10 per cent under the tutelage of coach Butch Harmon. Here, Scott and Harmon discuss the changes that they've made.

Butch Harmon: Adam's chipping action has become a little shorter; there's less wrist cock and more speed through the ball.
Adam Scott: I've been working at home on getting rid of the wrist cock because when you play chips with the wrists, it just isn't as consistent. I've found that firming up the wrists helps me strike the ball much better.
BH: The average player just stands too still and flips at it with his wrists.
AS: The thing is when you do it really well,

you can hit it so much harder than you think because it's going to pitch and stop.
BH: The key is you have to always accelerate, you can't slow down.
AS: I also really like the feeling of working the left knee forwards slightly because it keeps the weight on the left side.
BH: If the left knee moves towards the ball slightly on the takeaway, it means the weight has stayed on it, which is what you want. If it slides away from the target at all, that's because you will have moved too much weight onto the back foot and the danger is you're going to scoop.

• Now turn over for Adam's chipping drills.

PLAYING FROM A TIGHT LIE

Having worked hard on this shot, I now feel that I have so much more control – and that breeds confidence.

If there is any wrist cock here, then it is kept to an absolute minimum.

Keeping the backswing short is fundamental. Sometimes Butch stands with a club held out at hip height so that I can't take my wedge back too far.

I try and keep my right knee still so that my weight stays on the left side.

IMPACT

FOLLOWTHROUGH

Rather than thinking about getting speed with your arms or upper body, it becomes easier if you do it with the lower body. Still keep it very rhythmical.

I want to feel like I'm accelerating through the ball. You need that speed to give you the spin, control and commitment you are looking for.

I like to think about my knees in this shot. The left knee stayed solid in the backswing, but my right knee now drives through the shot.

No wrist hinge through the ball.

Only now have I allowed the club to rotate slightly.

It's the knees for me. I leave the left knee solid on the backswing to keep it short, and then drive the right knee through.

If you took a photo of me at impact, I'd want the club to look like it is at address. The loft should be exactly the same. Keep the wrists firm.

○ **MARTIN KAYMER**

THINK CREATIVELY
ROUND THE GREEN

A lot of players walk up to a ball near the putting surface and have one thought in their mind. They grab the same club and rely on the same chipping action to get them out of trouble every time. As a standard approach there is nothing much wrong with that, but it doesn't allow for any imagination – and creativity is the key to a great short game. Let me show you what I mean, with the help of a thick lie in greenside rough which you can treat like a trap shot. Free your mind and you might just add a new dimension to your short game.

At address you need the ball forward of centre with your hands either over it or slightly behind.

First step: read the lie

Look to see if the grass is growing in the direction of the shot or against it. When the grass is with you, then the ball will come out lower and not pop up quite as much so you may need to open the blade even more. If you are playing into the grain then square the blade up a touch and be prepared to hit it slightly harder.

THE BUNKER SHOT FROM THE ROUGH

What happens if you've been a little wayward and are now sitting down in the thicker and whispier rough? You hear people say, 'play it like a bunker shot' and that is good advice. These are flare shots and fun to play. Relish the challenge.

There's a lot more hand action in this shot. Really cock the wrists going back.

Keep the legs quiet here. You don't want to drive forward with the right knee as you might for a normal swing. Just keep everything very stable.

Remember to get that full high finish. This is a shot you must commit to – don't stop too soon. You want to release and flow through.

TURN YOUR SHORT GAME AROUND

How Mark Roe helped me see the short game light.

I went to all the best coaches, David Leadbetter, Butch Harmon, you name them, but none could explain the technique that would make me a better chipper. Then Mark Roe gave me a lesson, and it is no exaggeration to say it was a eureka moment. Now my technique is so much better, and is making all the difference in the world. Here, Mark reveals the new technique that has helped me regain top form.

Perfect touch
Improved short game form has helped Lee Westwood to contend on Tour.

SET-UP

The first thing I asked Lee to do was stand nearer the ball, says Mark Roe. When I say nearer, I mean it – six inches nearer. I wanted to get Lee's eyeline nearer the ball. Bringing him closer to the target line made him more upright. And this made the angle of the shaft at set-up more upright too; ideal for short chips.

LOFT

The loft on the club at set-up should be the same as the loft at impact. That is one of the golden keys of chipping. You don't want to increase or lose loft at any stage of the stroke because that will require your hands to work where they don't need to.

HINGE

On short chips the hands should be quiet, but on longer chips you can use more wrist hinge. But they must hinge correctly. Lee has it spot on here, but it wasn't always so. He drew the club back as for his full swing, rotating the hands and taking the club back inside the line.

Set-up loft at impact

Lee's wedge has the same loft at impact it had at address; in fact if the ball wasn't popping up in the air you'd almost think he was at address. Also, Lee's legs are now more passive; his hips haven't moved. That's great. You don't want your hips turning as you do in a full shot, you need stability here – a firm base – and Lee has it now.

Hips haven't moved, promoting greater stability

Pro Secrets

There should be no head movement at all, either side-to-side or up and down. Lee used to lose height slightly at impact, but we are working to improve that.

Post-impact

You can see just a little movement in the knees here which is fine. Being stable from the hips down doesn't mean you need to be completely rigid. There will always be a small element of weight transfer, but this should only be felt by a slight rocking of the knees.

Throughswing

Rotation kills backspin. The moment you start rotating the clubface, as for a full shot, you are going to lose backspin and therefore control. See how the toe of Lee's clubface has not turned over? He now maintains the club's loft after impact. There's no regular hand release.

COACH'S NOTES

Old face angle

Loft retained

This could be the greatest improvement in Lee's short game right here. The leading edge of the club shows that the loft from address has been retained. I've drawn a line on the picture (right) to show you where the leading edge used to be. He used to rotate the club, but he doesn't anymore. That's why he can spin the ball and that's why he is better now at accessing tight pins.

○ NICK DOUGHERTY

FOUR WAYS TO BETTER CHIPPING

Soften your hands
Grip the club really loosely. Think of the grip of your club as if it were a baby bird.

You can spot a bad chipper before he takes the club back. They hunch over the ball and grip the club too tightly. With their stroke they jab or stab at the ball. And yet, with these tips you might never duff the ball again.

Relaxed rhythm
Make sure your tempo is smooth the whole way through the stroke, especially at the bottom. Don't jab at the ball. Think smooth.

Stay over the ball
Keep your sternum over the golf ball, throughout the stroke. Amateurs tend to want to 'lift' the ball out, so the natural tendency is to lean back. That's when the trouble starts, as you'll make contact with the ground early.

Use the bounce
Many amateurs come in too steeply. This gives no margin for error; if you come in tight to the ball you skull it across the green; hit the turf first you'll duff it. Wedges are designed literally to bounce off the turf, so will permit a shallow angle of attack. This gives much more margin for error because even if you are a touch behind the ball, the club will still bounce and make contact.

MASTER THE
BUMP-AND-RUN

Picking the right shot at the right time is very important. I do have a tendency sometimes to grab the 60° lob wedge whatever the challenge I'm faced with. It's not always the percentage option. The bump-and-run makes for a safer and effective alternative.

I'm using an 8-iron, ball back of centre in the stance, with my hands forward — from there it's just all shoulders. Think of maintaining that triangle formed between the shoulders and the hands (inset).

Keep your wrists firm and make sure your weight is on the left side so that the club comes back to the same place every time. Move your weight about and you can hit this shot heavy.

○ ANTHONY WALL
NEVER DUFF ANOTHER CHIP!

Here's a brilliant little shot to play round the greens that is guaranteed to save you shots. I call it the 'fluff free chip' because the technique makes chunking the grass first a thing of the past.

The basic idea is to lift the heel of the club off the ground so that the toe is the lowest point. This means standing much closer to the ball so the club shaft is almost upright.

Keep your normal grip, but play the shot with something resembling your putting stroke (keeping the wrists firm). The ball should be slightly back in the stance with the hands just ahead of the ball.

You are playing the ball out of the toe, so it'll come out quietly with very little spin. This means that you should be thinking about holing the shot.

It's perfect out of slightly fluffy lies by the green – we're talking five or 10 yards – and because you are playing it out of the toe, there is no spin to worry about.

The ball will release straight at the hole – and hopefully even go straight in.

Make the shaft more upright to raise the heel up.

SAND
SECRETS

The Tour stars exhibit phenomenal ball flight and spin control from sand; but those impressive skills are built on the fundamentals needed by any standard of player. From the basics to advanced spin techniques, these tips will first help you reach a level of competence before giving you the tools to add that extra finesse to your sand play.

Building a workstation
I've drawn lines in the sand to create a foundation. This is my 'workstation', and you need to get this right before we move on. As you'll see, I still swing across the target line but not by much.

Target line

Swing Path

WHAT YOU ARE
TRYING TO ACHIEVE

You were probably taught to slice across the ball in sand, which meant it would kick to the right on landing. That's fun, but it's not much good to a pro, who needs a far more consistent approach.

Instead, we are looking to see the ball release like a putt when it lands and that means making it spin end-over-end and not sideways.

I have spent many hours working on this with my coach Pete Cowne, and we have developed a technique that makes it was possible to work the sand in such a way that you could make the ball spin on a vertical axis. Control from a bunker means moving the sand in the direction you want the ball to go.

1. See here how the old method channels sand off to the side like a plough in a field. This can only lead to sidespin and a lack of control.

2. Here the club is on a straighter line to the hole and as the club squares, sand is collected on the face and then thrown forward. We call this the 'ripple effect.'

It starts here – the set-up

To encourage the right move through the shot, Pete got me to re-position my left leg. From the regular stance (above left), just turn your foot and knee out. This helps the turn and gives you a feeling of standing more open, even though you remain square.

PRIME THE RIGHT RELEASE

Learning to execute the correct release is key. If you can't develop a way to put vertical spin on the ball then you won't reach your trap potential.

Put whatever loft you want on the club at address, as long as the toe is behind the heel. Then as you swing back, folding your right arm close to the body (inset), you want to make sure that the toe is still behind the heel as it is here. Some will say I've opened the face, but I haven't, I've just maintained the loft.

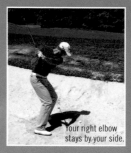

Your right elbow stays by your side.

1.

2.

As you release the club, think about keeping the butt of the grip aiming at your belt buckle so that the toe catches up with the heel just after impact. You are looking to square the club with the correct wrist hinge, arm speed and turn. This will ensure the bounce is used to take a nice shallow cut of sand. If you get too steep you won't get the bounce of the club working.

3.

The toe has overtaken the heel, but it's more down to correct body turn and release than because the hands have flipped over (see right). This scoops the sand and throws it at the hole; the ball follows.

Free the left shoulder

You must make sure that the left shoulder keeps moving up and out of the way through the shot. If it stops you'll to end up rotating the hands into a poor release (1). Allow the shoulder to clear and you'll be able to square up the club properly (2).

1. **X**

2. **✓**

Pro Secrets

With this technique you don't need to hit as hard. You don't hit across the line as much and are squaring the blade more, so less energy is lost.

THE SPLIT DRILL

A great drill I use frequently is to separate your hands on the grip. This helps ensure the clubhead is delivered correctly, so that the bounce works under the ball allowing the sand to ripple up the face and not away to the side.

Here you are pushing with your right hand and pulling back with the left, but you're not crossing over. Notice how my left shoulder keeps moving through the shot.

1.

2.

3.

LEARN TO 'WORK THE SAND'

Here's another great way to get accustomed to how the hands work through the swing, says Pete Cowen. Place them together in front of you, palms facing the ground. Then move them back, keeping the back of them pointing at your face. I've added sand and a ball here to give you the idea. Swing forward, keeping them parallel to you, so the sand and the ball are flung towards the target (2).

1.

2.

3.

A KILLER IN THE SAND

If there was one thing that I'd want you to learn from this article, it would be to get rid of shaft lean in the sand. If you lead with the hands in a bunker, you are just going to dig deep with the clubhead and lose control. Focus on the release we've shown you and, with practice, I think your bunker play will improve drastically.

FOCUS ON THE TARGET

My last thought before playing a bunker shot is not about the length of my swing, how I'm going to hinge my wrists or even how much sand I'm going to take – it is focused entirely on where I want the ball to land. I concentrate 100% on my target and that is where a lot of amateurs go wrong. They worry about technique when they should be worrying about where the ball is going. Technique is for the range; out on the course you need to play the game.

Let your lie dictate your shot

You can play a variety of shots from bunkers but a lot depends on your lie. If it's okay, I'll hit a lower shot by keeping the clubface square and moving the ball back into the middle of my stance. If I'm looking for more spin, I'll take less sand; if I want it to release, I'll take more.

TRY MY 'DOUGHNUT' GUIDE TO BETTER BUNKER PLAY

Next time you get into a bunker, just think that your ball is in the middle of a doughnut. It sounds strange I know, but it really does work. Concentrate on taking the same amount of sand with your stroke that you would need to make a doughnut.

As you walk into the sand, try to visualise this image rather than focusing on the ball. I have drawn a line around my ball here just to help that visualisation.

In pro-ams I see amateurs struggling away in bunkers. The problem stems from too many different thoughts; plus often their swing becomes too short and snatchy.

Just swing easily through the ball, thinking all the time about the doughnut. If you do this, you really can't fail to come out of any sort of bunker.

Finally, make sure you finish your follow-through. Don't stop on it. This will ensure the ball comes out with height to clear the lip, and lands gently on the green.

○ RICHARD STERNE

KEEP YOUR SPEED CONSTANT

If I was to give you one tip to help your bunker shots it would be to play them with good rhythm. By that I mean try and maintain a consistent swing speed throughout the shot. Yes, you need the clubhead to move quickly through the sand; but it should be achieved by an obvious acceleration.

Left side story

To help your rhythm, splay out your left foot slightly and point the knee down your shoe. Feeling some pressure in the thigh. This gives a stable base and helps you turn onto the ball the same way every time. This helps get your weight central without getting too much onto the left side.

FEAR-FREE TRAP PLAY

Before we get into the technique, there are two things you must do to give yourself your best chance of success. First, as you walk into the sand, imagine the shot you are about to play. Replay it in your head several times. Think about how hard you are going to hit it; picture exactly where the ball is going to land on the green, and how much it is going to release.

My five golden rules

Rule 1: At address, open up your stance in relation to the target and make sure the clubface is wide open too. You need to encourage the bounce on the club to work.

Rule 2: Keep my lower body as still as possible and concentrate on what's happening with your hands. The less body movement you have the easier it is to control the speed of your clubhead.

Rule 3: Keep your legs quiet too. That way you can be consistent with the amout of sand that you take.

Rule 4: Focus on a spot two inches behind the ball. This is where you want your clubface to make contact with the sand.

Rule 5: Make sure you accelerate through the ball. As we've said, you've got to be aggressive, even on short shots. Feel like you will throw the sand all the way onto the green.

See the divot
Next time you play a bunker shot remember to look at the channel you've blasted in the sand before you look up. ➡

Secondly, the most common mistake I see amateurs make in pro-ams is to quit on the shot. There is a deceleration rather than an acceleration. However short the distance is to the pin, you still have to be aggressive through the shot. Open up the face and take more sand; but always think about being aggressive.

The 'fried egg' lie

Always remember that what you are trying to achieve here is to get your ball on the green. Don't try to be too greedy.

When the ball is buried, I look to square up the clubface or even have it slightly closed so that it will knife under the ball. Many amateurs think you need to open the face even more; but in fact the reverse is true. When your club hits the sand, your face will automatically open.

You can see how I am making a narrower backswing with more wrist hinge here, which puts me more over the ball at impact. This is because I need to be steeper into the shot; more wrist break allows that.

Read the sand

Even on Tour the sort of sand we are faced with changes from week to week. As a loose guide, when the sand is wet and hard, you need to make a steeper swing and use a squarer face.

Going square

It's not just this plugged lie that requires you to square up that leading edge. Try this out of wet, hard sand too.

SPIN THE BALL FROM SAND

I have been working with Mark Roe on my trap play. When we started I was a very 'left-sided' bunker player; Mark doesn't believe you can play great bunker shots from your left side as it steepens your angle of attack and makes it tough to take sand consistently. So we worked on my set-up to get my weight more neutral. Mark also wanted to gain control of my wrist action to calm rotation and add hinge.

Takeaway 1

Takeaway 2

In being left sided, I tended to get too steep and would take too much sand. That stopped me being able to control spin. Now, with my weight centred, my backswing is wider, which helps shallow my angle of attack. That means less sand, more spin and more control.

Right angles
Lee's great hand position shows his wrists have hinged properly and not rotated; the clubface position shows he has retained his address loft.

Wide boy
Neutral set-up weight gives the backswing more width and helps Lee take a shallower sand divot.

MIRROR IMAGE

At the finish, if the clubface was a mirror, I'd want you to see your face in the reflection. It shows that from beginning to end you have retained the same loft on the club. Also, see how I am still not on my left side; I am neutral, and that is the way it should be.

Spin doctor
Lee's weight is neutral; the face hasn't rotated. The ball is loaded with backspin.

Great shots of impact here and what pleases me most is that you can clearly see I have not shifted my weight to the left side. My hands have released but NOT rotationally. Because I hinged my wrists correctly in the backswing, they've had the freedom to release down the line to the target. Look at the position of the clubface; there is no rotation there – that is your check point.

Impact

BALANCE A BALL TO USE BOUNCE

Amateurs are often frightened to open the clubface because they think it's a trick that only the pros can pull off. Next time you're in sand, try opening the clubface so that you can balance a ball on the face (A). From this position you are guaranteed to get the

natural bounce of the club to work. Practise skimming the club through the sand using that bounce. You don't want the club to dig too deep because then you lose control. A nice shallow divot (B) is what you're looking for so the ball gently lobs out.

Open the clubface and make a shallow divot to float the ball out of sand every time.

○ RORY MCILROY

LOB AND STOP FROM SAND

With a tight pin and little green to work with, the high explosive bunker shot that stops within a foot of landing is just the job.

I'll be honest with you, this is not for the faint-hearted! A normal bunker shot and you're looking to take the sand a couple of inches behind the ball, but here I like to get as close to the ball as possible. It's not an easy shot to execute but with practice it can be a very useful – and exciting – one.

Strengthen your left hand and weaken the right to keep the face open through impact.

This is a very handy shot. Look how the wrists work through to the finish.

Fan the blade wide open, even compared to a normal bunker shot position. It's almost as if a marble would roll backwards, away from the ball, if placed on the clubface.

I use my 60° wedge for this shot. It's not just for the loft; the sole plate has a nice curved camber which helps it cut smoothly through sand.

Your weight needs to be at least 60 per cent on the left side. I'm not sure you can swing too hard at this one.

ON THE GREEN

When it comes to technique, putting affords the most scope for versatility of any part of the game. That's why this section sees the widest variety of hints and tips. But these methods have at least one thing in common — they work for the Tour pros preaching them. So head to the practice green with a few balls and see which theory works for you.

Take aim

1. Place a ball 18 inches behind the hole. This is the point you should aim for, not the hole. Always aim to hit every putt past the hole to give it a chance of dropping.

TAKE A BREAK

I don't believe in hitting putts firm and straight into the hole. I think you sink far more putts by allowing for the break; I prefer to see my putts die into the hole. Most golfers under-read putts, so I'd recommend you practise on a slopy part of the practice green and always miss your putts on the high side, not the low side.

WATER SPILL

I've never had a problem reading greens; you just need a good eye for the slopes. Imagination is the key. Imagine a bucket of water being spilt across the putting surface and picture the direction in which the water would trickle.

Triangle

2. Set out golf balls in a triangle, starting closest to the hole with two balls five feet away. Work outwards, placing balls every three feet, making the triangle wider as you go. I generally set up the pyramid to about 20ft.

Putt

3. Starting at the closest ball, strike the putt and work backwards. You are working on pace, so we don't want any balls coming up short.

○ **PAUL LAWRIE**

BUILD YOUR
FEEL FOR SPEED

When you play on different courses week in week out, the speed of
the greens can vary quite a bit. Here's a drill I use to help me get
the pace of the greens on the Wednesday of a tournament week.

Relax

I use the reverse overlapping grip, and keep the pressure very light. You need to stay relaxed over the ball; gripping too tightly will make it very hard to swing smoothly.

Trigger

I push my hands slightly ahead of the ball just before I take the putter back. This forward press is a trigger for me to take the putter away smoothly. It forms part of my routine; by using it under pressure I'll still make a smooth stroke.

Eyes over the ball

One mistake I used to make was standing too close to my ball. Once I moved further away and got my eyes directly over the ball, I found it much easier to see the line.

On the left

Keep a little more weight on your left side at set-up. This encourages the putter to stay very low to the ground as it strikes the ball just beneath its equator, creating a smoother roll.

Feel drill

Putting three balls into a box made from four tees helps me gauge the speed of the greens.

○ LUKE DONALD

IMPROVE YOUR TOUCH PUTTING

Many amateurs warm up on the range for 30 minutes but forget green speed. It's a shame, because judgement of pace is critical to your score. Here's a drill I use that really helps my feel.

1. Use four tee pegs to mark out a box behind the hole. Use the length of your putter to create the length of the box's sides (inset). The hole lies on the front edge of the box.

2. Take three balls and set up to a putt 15 feet or so from the hole. Try to hole each one; but with the first one, you are looking to die the ball in the front edge of the cup. With the second give it a touch more, and with the third a little more again – though not so that you'll send it beyond the box.

3. You've completed the task when each putt is successively longer than the previous one – while staying inside the box. A holed putt always counts, whatever the pace.

4. Move back six feet, and repeat the drill. I will usually do this three-ball routine from four different distances, perhaps 15, 21, 27 and 33 feet, never moving back till I complete the previous one. Normally I can do the lot in about 15 minutes. Can you?

FOLLOW THE THIN BLUE LINE

Positive putting is all about finding a routine you are comfortable with, and sticking to it. Build in a couple of technical fundamentals and a positive mental attitude and you are set to hole a lot of putts.

SEEING IS BELIEVING

As part of my routine, I like to visualise a blue line that goes from my ball, all the way to the hole.

BALL MARK

I always use a blue marker pen on my ball because that blue sign triggers the blue line in my head. I place it on the ground so that I can see the mark clearly. Over the ball, I picture the entire line to the hole. I like to pick a spot in the hole, a blade of grass or a crack in the soil (here I've placed a tee in the hole to give you the idea). When I putt I try not to think about the hole; I just focus on rolling the ball down the line to the tee peg at the other end.

How my routine works

Once I get into my routine, I don't think about anything else. It's all a rehearsed procedure, and that really helps you to focus the same way on the job in hand whether it's a big pressure putt or not.

1. From the moment I place my left hand on the putter, I'm into my routine and I start to picture that blue line.

2. I follow it all the way to the hole, making sure my practice stroke mimics the real thing.

3. Over the ball I check that the face is square and that I'm lined up correctly. I then picture blue line once more.

4. I strike the putt as I've done thousands of times before.

THE SPINE IS THE KEY

When you swing the putter out in front of you like this, the spine provides the fulcrum to the turn. Your stroke is no different.

The natural arc

When lowering the putter to the ground, you will swing it along a slight arc. This is a natural path and the clubface should always be square to that curved line. I'm not a believer in the square-to-square method. Trying to keep the putter face to the target is an artificial stroke where the shoulders are moving unnaturally.

Pro Secrets

I try to be as relaxed as possible; you don't want to be worried about missing. Sure, if you've hit it to six feet you don't want to waste a good iron shot, but you have to block that sort of pressure out.

when I miss...
...it's not my fault

I hole a lot of putts from inside ten feet. But when one does slip by the hole, I try not to blame myself. My stroke is so ingrained now, I've practised it so much, that the chances of it being a fault are minimal. I would not regard a miss from ten feet as being my fault.

TRUST YOUR INSTINCT;
TRUST YOURSELF

If you are messing about on the practice green, you frequently read putts quickly then knock them dead weight into the middle of the hole. It is rare to be miles out with the initial read.

I always look from the ball to the hole and most of the time that will be it. There is a danger if you look from both sides that you will just confuse the read.

On long putts I move to the low side to get a better idea of pace.

○ DANNY WILLETT

HOW TO BOSS THE MOSS

These simple tips will help you knock long putts closer... and short ones into the hole.

Establish what is 'square'

You really need to understand what's square, as opposed to thinking what's square. I've done a lot of chalk line work to get a feel of what square is. I centre my set-up on my sternum (picture 1) and make sure my eyes are level over the ball – if your head dips, you're not square (2). From 12-15 feet in, unless you're set up square (3) you'll never hole out consistently.

My new grip

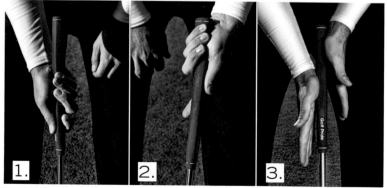

Many people have their thumbs on the front of the grip, but I like my lifelines on the grip, thumbs pointing down the shaft (1, 2). It feels very strange at first, but it's very neutral and it helps prevent the face twisting. I think of it as a split palm-to-palm grip. To get a feel for it, place your palms flat on the grip (3) and push inwards with each hand.

Amateur dramatics

I see lots of amateurs with a good stroke, but their approach is all wrong. Look at Tiger – possibly the best putter in the world. He approaches every putt as if he's going to hole it. A lot of amateurs will just walk up to it and say 'Yep, I like that, let's give it a go'. A bit more care can go a long way.

Path

I think you've got to arc the club a little. It's almost impossible to keep the face perfectly square-to-square if you're working the club from your centres.

Go with your instincts

As you mark the ball you'll have a glance at the contours and usually the line you see first is the correct one. I don't like a line on the ball, as some do. I've worked a lot on trusting what you feel and what you see – gut instinct.

For better lag putting, don't lag!

I'll start thinking about the putt as I walk up to the green; from further back you can see the slopes and breaks and get a better feel for them. The most important part of a long putt is the last six to eight feet – when the pace is dying off. I like to think about holing every putt. The worst thing you can do is try to lag it up there, because inevitably you're going to leave yourself six feet short.

○ **PADRAIG HARRINGTON**

WHY I PUTT CACK-HANDED

I've used this cack-handed grip with my putter for almost 10 years now. It's just a question of alignment – I actually have a better stroke when I use the conventional method but I line up much better when I use this reverse handed method.

1.

2.

Straight line
I feel I have a better stroke with a normal grip – but I set up squarer with left-below-right.

3.

4.

Comfort focus
Arrange your fingers in a light way that feels comfortable.

Side by side
Sit your thumbs next to each other to help keep your shoulders square throughout the stroke.

○JOHAN EDFORS

TRY MY TWO-THUMB GRIP TIP

I had a tendency to get open in the shoulders, which would lead to me pulling putts. I tried cross-handed for a while and that squared them up nicely, but it never felt comfortable. My coach suggested the grip that you see above. The club is held normally by the left hand, but rather than placing your right hand over the left, place it to the side of it so that only your thumbs and index fingers are touching the rubber. Apart from giving you a nice square stance, this grip also means that you can't grip the club too tightly.

KEEP YOUR STROKE SIMPLE

I wouldn't say I've noticed the greens being much faster on Tour – at least not yet, anyway. I keep my putting technique simple – if you complicate things, you'll lose some of your feel.

Palm to palm

Set your palms facing each other and it's easier to keep the club square.

Make a unit

I keep the left index finger on the grip to bind that palm to the clubface.

WHY I FOLLOW THE PRINCIPLE OF A SQUARE-TO-SQUARE STROKE

1. Working my hands down the target line, I try to keep the blade facing the hole for as long as I can. Keep wrists firm, rock the shoulders. Simple.

2. Indecision on the line of a putt can be fatal, so I always pick a spot about five inches in front of the ball and roll it over that, keeping the clubface square.

3. See how I'm holding the face on line. If I have a fault, I occasionally take the putter outside the line and impart hook spin, which will cause me to miss left.

KEEP A STEADY HEAD

Amateurs I play with are often amazed at how pros achieve so much consistent feel and accuracy with a putter; and yet to me it's the one part of the game which you can improve fast – especially armed with this useful steadying pointer.

1. Listen for the hole rattle

Look at the grass just behind your ball; wait until you hear your ball drop in the back of the hole before you look.

2. One pound coin drill

So many amateurs stare at their golf ball for hours as they are over a putt – and then move their head as the ball is about to be struck, compromising accuracy. I never focus directly on the ball when I am putting. I focus on the grass just behind the ball, something that is not about to move. To help you with this, put a £1 coin immediately behind the ball. Then place your blade behind the coin. Focus on the coin right through the stroke.

COIN FOCUS

The benefit of this focus is that it keeps your head down. So many amateurs look up too soon to see if their ball is going in the hole. When you take the coin away and play for real on the course, you will find yourself focusing on the piece of grass where the coin would normally be. And that holds your head steady.

BEATING
PRESSURE

Modern, powerful equipment and ever-lengthening courses have turned golf into a power game, with distance off the tee an increasingly valuable weapon. Here, the European Tour's elite share their secrets on the yard-munching techniques they use to propel the ball more than 300 yards on a regular basis – and without sacrificing control.

KEEP IT SIMPLE TO THWART PRESSURE

We all have a fear of pulling it left in the water or pushing it right in the trees; yes, even Tour pros. But when you're confident with your shot making, you can stand there and it doesn't matter if the whole green is surrounded by water. You can stand up there and hit it to a foot, because you're not thinking of anything else. When I get my confidence going, the only thing I see is the flag and I just go straight at it.

Unfortunately, though, this type of confidence is not something you can just turn on and off. It comes from developing a simple and repeatable method. I will run through the parts of my swing that plants the consistency from which pressure-beating confidence can grow.

A comfortable address position, but not a lazy one. It is easy to lose your discipline and become slumped, so that is to be avoided.

The clubhead is following a wide arc away from the ball and the right elbow is hinging nicely into the body.

The hips have returned to the address position, but the body is lagging behind allowing the club to stay on the inside. You can't rush the transition.

A fine example of extension through impact and a firm left side.

Three-quarters of the way back and you could say that the club is a little too steep at this point.

Slightly across the line at the top, but the shoulders have turned on a good plane.

Keeping a good spine angle past impact means that you have kept down on the shot rather than coming up out of it.

A good balanced finish is something that many amateurs would do well to copy.

○ IAN POULTER

PITCH CLOSE UNDER PRESSURE

I've never felt the incredible surge of adrenalin I experienced after making an up-and-down to win a fourball match in the 2008 Ryder Cup.

One-up playing the last, my 5-wood second shot was not great, but I knew being short of the hole still gave me a chance of making the up-and-down which would effectively win the match for us.

As I surveyed the 40-yard shot I was thinking solely about pitching it where I wanted to on the front of the green. I hit it pure. It pitched on the front of the green but didn't check up as much as I would have liked, so I was left with a nasty little three-footer. Thankfully, I managed to roll it in the middle.

Here are the pitching basics I use to play high-pressure shots like that one.

Visualise a landing spot
Pick an area about as big as a dustbin lid where your ball is going to land before releasing to the hole. After choosing this, I then just look at this rather than at the hole.

Feet close together
This enables you to get over the ball. So many amateurs I see have too much weight on their back foot, which means they end up trying to 'scoop' the ball. That's fatal. Yet you also don't want too much weight on the front foot. Just try to be nicely balanced.

Grip down to shorten the club
Pushing the hands slightly forward moves your weight to the front foot, promoting a nice, descending blow. Concentrate on taking the ball first, before the ground.

Swing back to 9 o'clock only
Amateurs often take too long a backswing on this shot. Don't go past horizontal. You don't have to make a big wrist-cock here.

Swing up and down the line
As you turn your hips and shoulders on the downswing, concentrate on holding the face square to the target (not allowing the toe of the club to overtake the heel during impact). In other words, hold off the release, as opposed to a normal shot where you allow your wrists to turn over.

Open stance
An open stance means my hips and body set-up is pointing slightly left of my target.

HOW TO HOLE CLUTCH PUTTS

I think holing out is a real strength of mine. I recall several I holed during the 2008 Ryder Cup matches; you can draw strength from those later in your career. I'm going to explain some of the things that keep me positive when the heat is on.

I've worked hard with my coach Clive Tucker. We've looked at my set-up, aim and eye position. I had a tendency to come up out of putts, especially on left-to-rights, so I work on making myself stay down and releasing the putter.

Fix the faults
Check #1

I used to get my hips too open because I'd be focusing very much on the hole. So I've worked on squaring them up to a line parallel to the target line. Having your hips or shoulders aligned poorly makes it very difficult to build a consistent stroke. You must check things like this frequently.

I like to breathe out just before I take the putter away. It's a good way to let pressure seep away. It relaxes the body and means you can move the club without tension. It also keeps you in the present and clears your head of mechanics.

Check #2

I have a tendency to have my hands too low at address, which can cause the heel to hit the ground and the face to close. so I've got into the habit of lining up the club so that it sits in a good upright position with the sole flat on the ground.

Check #3

I like to have the ball just off my left heel, which means my eyes are an inch or so inside the target line and slightly behind the ball. I check this all the time with a mirror on the green, just to make sure nothing has moved.

○ DR KARL MORRIS

HOW TO WORK ON
YOUR MIND GAME

Improve your thinking as well as your swing, says Tour psychologist Dr Karl Morris.

Consequence
Phil Mickelson must start again if one putt misses; this builds pressure.

Club golfers readily accept the need to work on your game physically, in terms of technique and fitness; not so many consider you can train the golf brain in the same, practical way. The trick is to know HOW to improve your mind to increase performance and results.

To do that, let us look at how golfers practise. In simple terms what we are trying to do when we change our swing is to make new neural connections in the brain. If we know what the brain 'likes' and 'dislikes' in terms of learning, we can make our practice far more effective.

Practise with... Attention
'Hit till your hands bleed' and 'Dig it out of the dirt' are two phrases we've accepted as the one true path to improvement. But neuro-science shows us that the key to effective practice is not the quantity but the quality – specifically the quality of your attention to your task. 45 minutes of quality focus and being absorbed in what you are doing is far better than trying to stay out there on Misery Hill until you have hit a certain number of balls or completed an allotted time.

Practise with... Consequence
A huge difference between practice and play is the element of consequence. Practice tends to be free of it;

yet on the course, the scorecard element means it's everywhere, adding a pressure we haven't trained to deal with.

For your brain to be able to handle a situation, you need to practise in an environment similar to the place you're put to the test. If we play a game of ultimate consequence, our practice must reflect that.

An effective way to add consequence is to set yourself practice drills that involve a score. Any time you recognise you are being tested, the consequence stakes are ramped up. The Par 18 game – throw nine balls around a green with an aim to up-and-down them all – is a brilliant way to recreate the pressure you feel on the links, with a scorecard in your back pocket.

Add emotion to your practice

In an experiment two unrelated groups were asked to view several movies. The control group was allowed to view the shows without restriction. The second group was instructed to observe the shows without any emotional response whatsoever. At the end both groups were asked questions to test recall.

Every member of the control group who experienced emotional responses remembered the details of each movie to a far greater degree.

If we want to be able to recall skills in the future, it makes sense to put some emotion into the things that we do well. Even during practice, when you hit a

great shot or hole a good putt, instead of the usual ho-hum response allow yourself either internally or externally to get 'high' on the success. Allowing yourself the privilege of emotion could well help your brain remind you of what you are capable when you face a similar shot under pressure on the course.

BEING IN THE BUBBLE

A mental tip I find useful with chipping is to separate the preparation from the execution. If you do that successfully, you'll find that you can be much more relaxed over the ball and will be less likely to worry about where it goes. Let me explain.

For any chip shot, your first task is to picture the shot. See the ball in the air, find a landing spot and make a judgement on how it will roll up to the hole.

Once you've selected the shot you want to play, you need to forget about the hole. Just execute the shot that is required. Free from the stress of working out what you need to do over the ball, you can relax and play the shot required.

I've found this approach very effective; but if the shot doesn't come off, you need to either improve your technique or your judgement of the right shot selection.

Full focus
I manage what's in the bubble, not what is outside.

MAKE THOSE CLUTCH PUTTS

The two most pressure-packed putts of my career both came in 2008.

The first was at the Open. It was an 18-footer and, at the time, I thought if I could make it I might win the Claret Jug. Even though there were 20,000 people around the hole and millions watching on TV, I didn't really notice them because I was concentrating so hard on the line. Although I was probably over the ball for only about 15 seconds, it felt like a lifetime, and yet I just tried to enjoy it. It went right in the middle.

The second came in Ryder Cup that September during the Saturday fourballs with Graeme McDowell against Jim Furyk and Kenny Perry. It was the best match I've ever played in. They were five under for the last seven holes, but I still had a putt on the last to win. It was only three feet, but the whole match depended on it, and it was a fast downhiller.

As soon as I marked my putt I could see the line: just left of centre. Provided I hit that line, it was going to go in because it was so fast. When it went in I went bananas.

Here, I'll share with you some of the secrets that helped me stay calm under pressure.

Breathe properly
Everything is telling you to get over-excited, but if you focus on breathing slowly and deeply, you can counter this.

Enjoy the pressure
Get excited, not nervous. Don't think about the repercussions of missing the putt; think about what's going to happen when you make it.

Take your time
You might find yourself rushing your preparation and your walking. Just think about slowing it all down.

Pick the right line
Without this, it's not going to go in. Look from both sides of the hole and don't get over the ball until you are quite sure of the line and have visualised the ball falling in the hole.

Keep focused
So many amateurs I see in pro-ams get sidetracked by all the peripheral things around them. Just keep visualising the ball rolling into the middle of the hole on the perfect line and with perfect pace.

TOUR
TECHNIQUE

The typical modern Tour pro is an athlete – tall, supple and able to propel the ball mighty distances. But that doesn't mean they have different swing issues to ordinary mortals. The Tour pro's golf swing must obey the same laws of physics as yours and mine, and that's why their problems are also ours. Naturally, their solutions are too.

KEEP IT UNDER
THE WIND

You need to think low to play low. Learning to hit the ball with a lower trajectory was one of the first challenges I faced when I arrived on tour. The English guys, like Simon Dyson, were all good at it, but in South Africa, I'd been used to playing with a higher ball flight.

There are three things I do to get the ball to fly under the wind.

1. I visualise the shot I want to hit. If you see a lower flight and picture a flatter trajectory, then your natural instinct will help you to execute it successfully. This might sound odd, but give it a try.

2. I tee the ball a little lower. This is because I'm looking to sweep the ball off the top of the tee peg at the bottom of my arc. I'm not trying to hit 'up' the back of the ball.

3. I employ a slower rhythm. If you hit fiercely at the ball then you'll struggle to keep it down. Just make your rhythm nice and smooth. This doesn't mean shortening your swing, because all that does is encourage you to get too quick from the top.

For a low drive I start by visualising a low shot; then I tee it lower and slow down my swing.

HIGH

LOW

PLANE IMPROVER

Last season I had a problem taking the club away too much on the outside and on too steep a plane. At address my hands were positioned as they are in picture A, centrally in my posture.

Moving them forward as they are in picture B has helped me to take the club on a much better plane going back so that it remains square throughout. Now all I need to do is turn back and through the shot.

A

B

My tip with the driver is to have a wide stance, but not one that hinders your turn or makes weight transfer an issue.

This is a great position with the club marginally outside the line of the hands. I'm nicely on plane here rather than being too steep in the takeaway. If you get the club off plane early (inset) then you have to fight to get back in position.

Again, I'd have to be pleased with the plane here, since it is very much on the same plane coming back into the ball as it was moving away.

When players talk about being in 'the slot', they mean they are not fighting a fault with their hands. When you have the club in a good position you are free to hit hard through the ball, as I am here.

Fully coiled and ready to go, but you must let your natural rhythm dictate the pace of transition.

I've just turning my left shoulder and arm. I'm now on a flatter plane, the shaft tracing a line through to the ball.

I've had no need to hold the face off here because I've been able to swing nicely down the line.

If you release power at the right time there is no reason why you can't maintain a balanced finish.

Pro Secrets

You need your energy levels to be high when you work on your driver. Try not to go to the range when you are feeling tired.

HOW I TURNED A LOW FADE INTO A HIGH DRAW

When I first arrived on Tour, if you'd asked me to hit a high draw it wouldn't have been a comfortable shot for me. I tended to hit the ball very low and, although I could move it both ways, my natural shape was definitely a fade.

Now, I'm not a very technical player so I said to my coach Kevin Smeltz that each time I saw him, I just wanted one small thing that would make me better. For me, a swing change is something that has to happen very gradually. It would have been too much of a risk for me to tear up what I was doing and start again from scratch.

'Camilo wanted to be able to hit the high draw,' says Smeltz, 'but he was never going to achieve that with the way he swung the club – his weight was back at address, his hands moved away from his body on the downswing and exited to the left after impact. When he said he could hit a draw, it was more of a pull draw with the club coming from outside the target line. I knew what we had to do but we set about changing his swing one step at a time.'

POSTURE CAME FIRST

I've worked on 'tilting' my pelvis a little more at address so the belt buckle is now fractionally below the tail bone. This angle helps me take the club away on a steeper arc, the first key move for me to hit a draw.

LEFT SIDE LOW

Here you can see how an improved posture has led to a better takeaway. The left shoulder and the left hip are lower than they used to be and this means that I'm now able to keep the club closer to the body through the swing.

I used to have my weight too much on the heels, which encouraged a poor takeaway that would be too low and around my body. I'm trying all the time to stand as tall as I can to the ball with my weight more on the balls of my feet and my chin higher. It's a much more athletic feel.

HIGHER HANDS AT THE TOP

I have a higher hand position at the top now and the
plane of the swing is such that the path of the downswing
is going to be much more where I need it to be.

My hands are now higher
at the top – and I'm
primed in a position to
swing down to impact in
exactly the way I want.

Pro Secrets

My hip turn was too level, meaning I'd
take the club away on a flat plane. It
meant I was unable to stay on the
inside before impact – something you
need for a proper draw.

KEEPING THE
HANDS CLOSE

Rather than working away from my body on
the downswing, my hands are now in a far
better position. This means that I can attack
the ball more from the inside and get a
much more solid strike.

Pro Secrets

'I think a lot of players can learn
from Camilo's approach mentally,'
says Kevin Smeltz. 'He very rarely
blames his swing for anything. If
he hasn't played well he'll just tell
me his attitude was wrong. He
won't make comments like, 'I
can't hit that shot' or 'My swing
was rubbish'. He knows that
such thoughts can only harm
his confidence.'

My hands are closer
to my body than they used
to be and I'm now ready to
attack the ball on the
necessary inside path to
produce a draw.

AT IMPACT

I now have great stability in my legs at impact. I used to have a flatter turn and too much leg slide to the target, so I got ahead of myself (inset). This caused a move across the ball at impact. Now my left leg is much straighter and I can hit up against that side.

See the difference between the left leg positions? Keeping tall in the posture at the start has helped me to stay tall through the ball, keeping that left leg straigher and more stable.

My hands are now not leading the club into the ball so much. I'm keeping the natural loft on the club, which gives me that higher flight I want.

HANDS EXIT HIGH

You only have to look at the position of the shaft to see I'm now able to exit much straighter and higher through impact, rather than dragging the club round my body to the left.

USE GLOVES FOR A BETTER TURN

Hands in front
Halfway back and my hands are still opposite my chest and in sync with my backswing turn.

I have a habit of moving the arms and club away from the ball without turning the body. This means I'm immediately out of sync, get ahead with my upper body on the way down and lose the shot to the right.

A drill I use is to put a golf glove under each arm and then hit shots making sure that the gloves are clamped firmly in place. This forces me to work my body, arms and club away from the ball in one go.

At address
Placing a glove under each arm is a simple way of ensuring you move your body and arms away in one piece.

FORWARD THINKING

I carry this yellow stick everywhere I go because as a practice aid there is nothing better. I could give you any number of uses, from laying it on the ground as an alignment aid to checking out the plane of your swing. Here, though, I'm using it to encourage the correct move on the downswing. Placing the stick a couple of inches outside my left foot, I think about trying to brush against it with my knee as I start the downswing. This helps me to concentrate on transferring my weight properly and clearing my hips.

On the move

My knee brushing the yellow stick is proof that I've transferred my weight properly.

Magic wand

Set your cane up a couple of inches outside your front foot, ready to monitor your left knee movement on the way down.

100

◯ HENRIK STENSON

ONE GOOD TURN

I'd been struggling for consistency for some time when, with the help of Pete Cowen, I traced my problem to the right hip. I hadn't been getting into my right hip enough in the backswing. If the hip doesn't get back far enough it can lead to a string of other problems, particularly in the longer clubs. Your upper body, arms and legs can get out of sync which is always going to spell trouble. Here's how we cured the problem:

Hip rotates

You can see in the main picture here that I've really cranked the right hip back and away from the ball, allowing me to complete the backswing more easily. It also gives me the space I need to drop the club down into the ideal hitting position as I move into impact. With the right hip locked (above), I no longer have that room.

Coil drill

Here's a drill I use that gets my body into a much better position in the backswing. It might look like a dance move and, I suppose, in some ways it is. But lifting the right elbow high, while pushing down with the left palm, really forces the hips and shoulders to coil back into a powerful, fully-wound position. Doing this without a club focuses your attention on where it needs to be, ensuring you don't get lazy in your posture.

Search back to the root cause

When you're trying to cure a fault you can play decent golf with the odd temporary fix, but when they get too many, you have to go back to the main crux of the problem. If you're not careful, you can end up making a host of compensations that eventually catch up with you. A series of errors can be cured by finding the underlying problem.

HOW TO CONTROL YOUR BALL FLIGHT

I had a spell some years ago where I could hardly get the thing airborne. I was getting my timing all wrong and either catching the ball heavy or thinning it.

My coach Pete Cowen took a look at my swing and we studied the video footage before he came up with a drill to rectify the problem. It has really transformed my game, giving me a much better ball flight, and one that is better suited to modern equipment.

Clubface too shut
This was my old takeaway. The clubface, was shut, meaning I was de-lofting the club.

A much better angle
Here's where I want to be. Notice the angle of the clubhead here with the toe pointing to the sky.

Left wrist bowed
I had a habit of bowing the wrist at the top which tended to make the clubface point to the sky – very closed.

Now there's more cupping
This is better. There's more cupping of the wrist here which is helping me to keep the loft on the club.

THE WAGGLING ROUTINE I USE

So those are the changes I've made. But I achieved them by taking three simple steps:

1. It's the waggle that matters. I start by setting up squarely to the ball as usual.

2. Then I waggle the club and replace it with the clubface in an open position.

3. This move puts loft on the club before I start the swing. But more importantly than that, it gets my hands in that much better position at the top of the backswing. Turn over to see how it works during the swing.

'Cupping' makes the difference

Look first at the top of the backswing. See how the toe of the club is pointing straight down? That is because I've now added much more loft and the club is in what would be considered an open position. You can 'cup' the left wrist quite excessively and still strike the ball well because it's impossible to keep it in the cupped position through impact.

SYNC UP TO KILL A HOOK

People often refer to me as a 'natural' looking player, but that doesn't mean I don't understand technique. For instance, I know I have a tendency to move the club too much on the inside as I go back. This would flatten the plane and lead me to get too deep (stuck behind me) on the way into impact. It costs me synchronisation as my body gets ahead of my hands, leaving them trapped with nowhere to go. Then two things can happen: my body will try to delay its turn by sliding the hips forwards, and my hands will try to catch up by rotating through the shot too quickly, possibly causing a hook.

My hips have moved ahead and are now sliding to allow my hands to catch up.

The hands have had to work too hard and have flipped over too quickly. Result: hook.

I keep my hands in front, so they stay synchronised with my hips.

My hands stay quieter; I can get better extension through impact.

○ ANTON HAIG

KEEP ON PLANE

When players talk about keeping the club in front of the body, the first two frames show that well.

My work on the range has been trying not to let the club get caught behind me. Sometimes I pick it up a little outside and then get behind my body.

Cocking my wrists quite early sets the club on a good plane and then I try and go straight up into a good high hands position at the top of the backswing.

You don't want to rush the transition, just drop your hands back down before releasing through impact.

Sometimes you get on the course and it feels a bit different, but you've got to keep grinding. I know it'll come good in the end.

Compare the images above and below: the positions are similar, showing how the hands have dropped the club down into the slot.

Maintaining the flex in the right knee at the top of the backswing is key to a good leg action.

The spine angle stays consistent right through the swing, vital for a good plane.

Technically, the right knee here has worked out a little too much towards the ball.

A perfect, balanced finish, something we should all be trying to achieve every shot.

BUILD A BETTER TAKEAWAY

I knew I had some technical issues with the first part of the swing, but I've worked hard over the years to create consistency and control. Use my improvements to help your game.

✗ Old swing
Set-up is so important. I'm hunched over and round shouldered here; I just can't swing back with athleticism and on a good path from this position.

✓ New swing
This is much better; a good spine angle and shoulders are back. You can't afford to be tired or lazy: you have to get this right before you move to the next stage.

✗ Old swing

Leading the swing with the arms, I've still got
the club a little shut here. I can still hit good shots
from here, but it becomes more difficult. Having a
closed face at the start means I have to save it later.

✓ New swing

I like the clubhead to move first, then the
wrists start to break, followed by the forearms and
body. The club is now square and I'm
in a position already to hit any shot I want.

1.

Perfect posture

So often, amateurs have great posture at address, but then lose it during the swing. On the range you will often see me with a tee in my mouth. I aim this at the ball throughout my swing; it helps keep my spine angle the same and prevent swaying.

○ OLIVER WILSON

PRACTICE MAKES PERFECT

Here are four simple practice drills from the tee to the green which can take shots off your game.

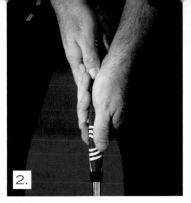

2.

Go left-hand-low to square up

Amateurs often set up with open shoulders on putts. Because their right hand is too much on top of the putter grip, their right shoulder is forced in front of the left; it can often lead to pulling your putts. An easy way round this is to start putting with your left hand below your right (right-handers) – even if only in practice. It immediately squares the shoulders.

3.

Left-hand-only chipping

Bad chipping is caused by deceleration and a lack of trust. I often practise using my left hand only; when I put the right back on, I try to maintain that feeling of the left hand dominating. If you trust the clubface loft to get the ball in the air, rather than trying to 'lift' it with your wrists, you'll turn through with acceleration.

4.

High tee to beat a slice

Tape a tee peg onto an old shaft or pole, and hit a ball from this height. This will force a flatter swing plane and encourage you to release the club and hit a draw. You should try and sweep the ball away without striking the tee; with a flat swing, your shoulders will turn around your body in one motion. This really is a wonderful way to stop the horrible over-the-top swing path which causes so many people to slice the ball.

Follow through
Good finish, standing on the right toe, 100 per cent of your weight on the left side.

Walk through
I won three tournaments in a row, coming from seven behind Watson in the first, seven behind Ballesteros in the second and six back from Andy Bean. I won those three because I wanted to get away from the reverse C. So I walked after every shot to be sure I didn't stay back on the ball.

○ **GARY PLAYER**

GET THROUGH THE BALL

What does every good player do? They get through the ball. I never saw a great player hanging back. They all have mass, and they move it forwards. A shot putter winds up and then leaps forward. Javelin is the same. Tennis players lean into the shot. Amateurs lean back on it. Staying behind the ball and posing in a big reverse C gives no power and a sore back. You've got to rotate.

STAYING ON PLANE

I used to teach weekend golfers and they all lay the club off at the top (shaft points left). It should aim at the target at the top. Do it and you'll be amazed by the improvement.

The cancer of golf is anytime you go outside the line. Go that side you become laid off.

Target line
Lay a club on the ground parallel to your target line and watch where you swing in relation to that.

Left arm/chest connection
Hogan said something I always remembered: you've got to hit the inside of the ball, not the outside. The left arm has to stay connected to the chest to achieve that. Lose connection and you'll reach the top laid off, start down outside the line and cut across the ball.

PLAYER GUIDE

Robert Allenby
Australian; US Tour player; turned pro 1991;
Presidents Cup team member

Paul Casey
English; European and US Tour player;
turned pro 2000; Ryder Cup team member

Darren Clarke
Northern Irish; European Tour player; Ryder
Cup team member

Luke Donald
English; European and US Tour player;
turned pro 2001; Ryder Cup team member

Nick Dougherty
English; European Tour player;
turned pro 2001

Bradley Dredge
Welsh; European Tour player; turned
pro 1996

Simon Dyson
English; European Tour player; turned pro
1999; Walker Cup team member 1999

Johan Edfors
Swedish; European Tour player;
turned pro 1997

Niclas Fasth
Swedish; European and US Tour player;
turned pro 1993; Ryder Cup team member

Anton Haig
South African; European and Asian Tour
player; turned pro 2004

Peter Hanson
Swedish; European Tour player;
turned pro 1998

Padraig Harrington
Irish; European and US Tour player; turned
pro 1995; Open Champion 2007, 2008; US
PGA Champion 2008; Ryder Cup team
member; European Tour Order of Merit
winner 2006

David Howell
English; European Tour player; turned pro
1995; Ryder Cup team member

Mikko Ilonen
Finnish; European Tour player;
turned pro 2001

Miguel Angel Jimenez
Spanish; European Tour player; turned pro
1982; Ryder Cup team member

Robert Karlsson
Swedish; European Tour player; turned pro
1989; Ryder Cup team member; European
Tour Order of Merit winner 2008

Martin Kaymer
German; European Tour player;
turned pro 2005

Simon Khan
English; European Tour player;
turned pro 1991

Paul Lawrie

Scottish; European Tour player; turned pro 1986; Open Champion 1999; Ryder Cup team member

Graeme McDowell

Northern Irish; European Tour player; turned pro 2002; Walker Cup team member 2001; Ryder Cup team member

Paul McGinley

Irish; European Tour player; turned pro 1991; Ryder Cup team member

Rory McIlroy

Northern Irish; European Tour player; turned pro 2007; Walker Cup team member 2007

Gary Player

South African; US, Southern Africa 'Sunshine' and Australasian Tour player; turned pro 1953; Open Champion 1959, 1968 and 1974; US Masters Champion 1961, 1974 and 1978; US PGA Champion 1962 and 1972; US Open Champion 1965; President's Cup team captain

Ian Poulter

English; European and US Tour player; turned pro 1995; Ryder Cup team member

Alvaro Quiros

Spanish; European Tour player; turned pro 2004

Charl Schwartzel

South African; European and 'Sunshine' Tour player; turned pro 2002

Adam Scott

Australian; European and US Tour player; turned pro 2000; Presidents Cup team member

Jeev Milkha Singh

Indian; European and Asian Tour player; turned pro 1993

Henrik Stenson

Swedish; European Tour player; turned pro 1998; Ryder Cup team member

Richard Sterne

South African; European and 'Sunshine' Tour player; turned pro 2001

Anthony Wall

English; European Tour player; turned pro 1995

Marc Warren

Scottish; European Tour player; turned pro 2002; Walker Cup team member 2001

Lee Westwood

English; European Tour player; turned pro 1993; Ryder Cup team member; European Tour Order of Merit winner 2000

Danny Willett

English European Tour player; turned pro 2008

Oliver Wilson

English; European Tour player; turned pro 2003; Walker Cup team member 2003; Ryder Cup team member

Ian Woosnam

Welsh; European Tour player; turned pro 1976; US Masters Champion 1991; Ryder Cup team member

Camilo Villegas

Colombian; US and European Tour player; turned pro 2004